The answer to *nearly* everything is PLAY

A treasure trove of ideas for supporting childhood development

ANNE MAREE TANEY

First published by Ultimate World Publishing 2024
Copyright © 2024 Anne Maree Taney

ISBN

Paperback: 978-1-923255-48-7
Ebook: 978-1-923255-49-4

Anne Maree Taney has asserted her rights under the Copyright, Designs and Patents Act 1988 to be identified as the author of this work. The information in this book is based on the author's experiences and opinions. The publisher specifically disclaims responsibility for any adverse consequences which may result from use of the information contained herein. Permission to use information has been sought by the author. Any breaches will be rectified in further editions of the book.

All rights reserved. No part of this publication may be reproduced, stored in or introduced into a retrieval system, or transmitted in any form, or by any means (electronic, mechanical, photocopying, recording or otherwise) without the prior written permission of the author. Any person who does any unauthorised act in relation to this publication may be liable to criminal prosecution and civil claims for damages. Enquiries should be made through the publisher.

Cover design: Ultimate World Publishing
Layout and typesetting: Ultimate World Publishing
Editor: Marinda Wilkinson

Ultimate World Publishing
Diamond Creek,
Victoria Australia 3089
www.writeabook.com.au

Dedication

I dedicate this book to all the families out there who are doing the best that they can with the resources available to them. You are amazing!

And to my family for all their love and support.

Acknowledgement of Country

I respectfully acknowledge the Gkuthaarn and Kukatj people as the Traditional Custodians of the land on which this book was written.

I recognise and honour their wisdom, strength and resilience and pay my respects to Elders, past, present and emerging. I acknowledge that the land was never ceded and always was, and always will be, Aboriginal land.

The ideas in this book do not replace professional advice about ways to support your child's development.

Contents

Dedication	iii
Acknowledgement of Country	v
Disclaimer	vii
Introduction	1
Chapter 1: It is not just fun and games!	7
Chapter 2: Pregnant and playful	21
Chapter 3: Connect the dots	39
Chapter 4: Catch me if you can!	55
Chapter 5: Giggles and goosebumps	75
Chapter 6: Fact and fiction	93
About the Author	107

Introduction

I initially set out on this book-writing adventure because I saw the need for a resource for parents who were concerned about their child's development. There are often long waits for an appointment with a paediatrician or other specialist services, and there is no advice about what to do in the interim. This can lead to frustration and feelings of helplessness.

Long waiting times and a lack of affordable services affect many children and families. The Australian Early Development Census data highlights the high level of need in Australia, showing that 1 in 5 students starting school are vulnerable in at least one domain. In some areas, this number rises to over half of our children (Department of Education, Skills and Employment, 2022). This problem is not unique to Australia but is repeated throughout the world. This needs to change!

The answer to nearly everything is PLAY

If a child's development is delayed when they start school, they are at risk of struggling academically and potentially developing social or emotional issues. These often translate into, or are interpreted as, behavioural issues. Ongoing behavioural issues can damage a child's reputation and their view of themselves, causing long-term disadvantage.

The good news is that there are things you can do! While you should not put off seeking a referral if you are concerned about your child — and having some strategies should not stop us from advocating for more services — play is a fun and connected way to aid your child's development while you wait.

As the book journey continued and I talked to more parents and carers, I realised that these play suggestions would also be helpful for many others. With less play available to kids and continually increasing family stressors, promoting play and playfulness has

Introduction

never been more important. Playful activities can reduce stress, increase social connection, boost creativity and release endorphins which improve mood. We all need some of that!

Other parents have told me they are searching for ways to reduce their child's device usage. These devices are (almost) essential to life these days, but staying the master of the machine rather than being enslaved by them is very challenging. It is challenging for adults, too. Devices are very addictive. A 'stop it' approach does not work. You need to swap it for another enjoyable activity so the brain still gets its dopamine boost. But what can you do? These lists will give you some ideas.

I hope this book will help many children and families connect and build skills through the magic of play. While 'free play' is the Ferrari (or Land Cruiser) in terms of play, I have found that targeted play, combined with connection, unconditional positive regard and a good dash of fun, is the ingredient of change when kids struggle with specific skills. The book's first chapter is all about play, the different types and their benefits. It's not just fun and games!

The next section of the book is devoted to the pregnant mum and her important role in caring for the resilient but vulnerable little life inside her. Safety, good health and a generous splash of play and playfulness are essential to mum's wellbeing and her unborn baby's healthy development.

Then it is time for some serious fun – or probably more accurately – some seriousness and some fun. The chapters are arranged according to a bottom-up brain development model (i.e. first, the brainstem, then the diencephalon and cerebellum, the limbic system and finally, the cortex). Where they fit together quite neatly, they are linked to the developmental domains used by the Australian Early Development Census. The domains they use are physical health, social competence, emotional maturity, language and cognitive skills and communication. This will allow you to quickly find the section of the book you require.

Each chapter includes information about that brain region, followed by games and play activities that support its development. The activity you offer must be appropriate for the child's developmental stage, not their age. They also must enjoy the activity. There may be sensory reasons why a child does not want to engage in a particular sort of play, or it may be too hard for them, too easy or 'boring', or it may just be a personal preference. Forcing a child to do activities they do not enjoy can damage your relationship and be ineffective in achieving your goals. Play must be fun! Chapter 4 has a section on adapting play for sensory needs.

Introduction

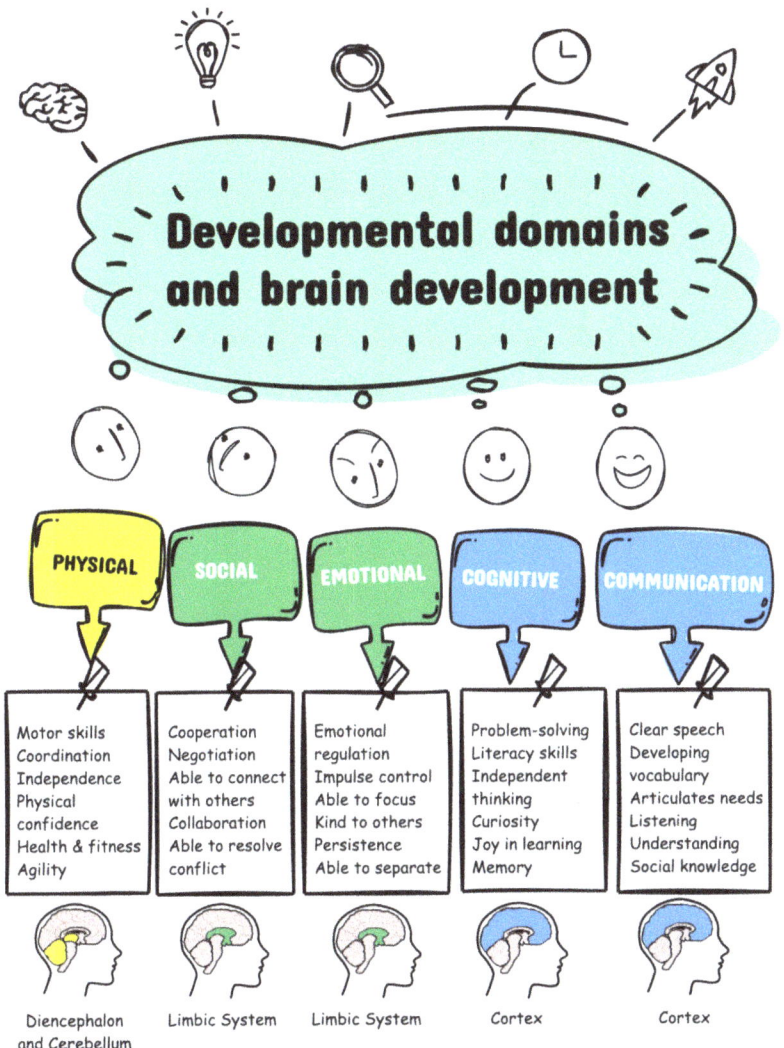

*This is only a model to visualise the complex brain development process and categorise skills. Many parts of the brain are used in every action we take and every thought we think.

When reading these chapters, remember that while I have used a bottom-up brain development model, all models of brain development are very simplified ways of explaining highly complex processes. Multiple areas of the brain are connected and involved

The answer to nearly everything is PLAY

in any activity, so some activities will be included in more than one area, but the focus will be different. Also, remember that while each area of the brain has periods of most rapid development, the brain continues to develop throughout life.

Even when things are difficult, engaging in play provides connection, skills, joy and hope. Play is the answer to (nearly) everything!

So, pack a picnic lunch and join this adventure in play. Don't expect to be back before dark. There is way more fun than that!

References

Department of Education, Skills and Employment. (2022). *Australian Early Development Census National Report 2021.* Department of Education, Skills and Employment. https://www.aedc.gov.au/resources/detail/2021-aedc-national-report

CHAPTER 1

It is not just fun and games!

When we see kids playing, it seems so natural and 'every day' – so every day, that often, we do not see its enormous value. Through their play, children are gaining the skills they need for life. They build healthy bodies and brains and process the events in their lives without any input from us. They learn to get on with others, regulate their emotions and gain problem-solving skills. It is not just fun and games! Play is essential to children's development.

Free play

Free play is supercharged! It is what children do when they are left to their own devices. The players, not the adults, organise free play; it is imaginative and has no planned goal (Howard, 2006). It takes twists and turns and evolves as it goes. Players need to negotiate the rules and roles and will likely combine many different types of play within one game. Most importantly, it is fun! The more opportunities you can give your child to experience this type of play, the better. It is one of life's most valuable gifts.

It is not just fun and games!

The amount of free play available to children has changed over the years. Safety concerns, families working long hours to survive economically, and the increased use of technology are some contributing factors. Reduced play in early childhood and preschool settings, with an increased focus on formal learning, has also impacted children's opportunities for free play. Even when there is play-based learning, there is often a deficit of free play.

Knowing the benefits means we can work on changing the balance for the benefit of *our* kids – and future generations. We can do this by prioritising play in our homes and community and advocating for more play, especially free play, in early learning environments.

'Play, in all its varieties taken together, works to build us into fully functioning, effective human beings.'
- Peter Grey

Play skills and targeted play

While working with young children, I have observed that many who are referred for behavioural, social or emotional reasons have play skills below what would be expected for their chronological age. Of course, a child may have these difficulties for many reasons other than a lack of play skills – and a range of developmental and other issues may also result in a lack of these skills. While this is a circular issue, play provides a fun, connected and essential way to support the development of typically developing kids. It can also help those struggling with skill development while waiting for specialist advice. If your child is waiting for an appointment, your increased knowledge about the benefits of play will be reassuring as you will know you are supporting their development in the best way possible. This can stave off the feelings of helplessness that can easily creep in when you are worried.

The following chapters include ideas for play that support childhood development across all the domains. While free play is ideal, targeted play has many benefits in filling developmental gaps and meeting learning goals. However, it must always remain fun and playful.

It is not just fun and games!

Check out the intense focus of these children and the way they are in sync with one another. It is fascinating to watch the wiring of little brains connect through play!

Types of play

As we start this quest into the wonders of play, let's look at some of the different types and their benefits. This is not an exhaustive list, but it gives you an idea of the immense value of everyday play. Often, you do not need to do anything different; instead, you need to recognise and understand the value of what you are already doing and offering.

Pretend play
- Stimulates the imagination.
- Requires problem-solving skills.
- Allows for processing of life events.
- Increases narrative language.
- Uses emotional regulation.

The answer to nearly everything is PLAY

Physical play
- Builds muscles and strengthens bones.
- Improves balance and coordination.
- Reduces stress.
- Increases social skills.

Rough-and-tumble play
- Provides opportunities to learn about boundaries.
- Practises emotional and behavioural regulation.
- Develops impulse control.

In rough-and-tumble play, children practise impulse control and emotional regulation. They also learn to read body language, assess risk and manage boundaries.

Games with rules
- Practises following rules and playing fairly.
- Promotes strategic thinking.

Cognitive play
- Practises focusing attention.
- Promotes logical and strategic thinking.
- Uses problem-solving skills.

Fantasy play
- Develops creativity.
- Helps children to understand what is real and what is not.
- Uses problem-solving skills.

Solitary play
- Develops their own unique interests and skills.
- Allows space to try new things.
- Promotes independence.

Construction play
- Develops fine motor skills.
- Improves hand-eye coordination and spatial awareness.

Sensorimotor play
- Stimulates the senses and develops sensory awareness.
- Promotes exploration and curiosity.
- Develops coordination and balance.

Social play
- Promotes sharing.
- Provides experiences of winning and losing.
- Develops empathy.
- Promotes consideration of other's thoughts and ideas.

The answer to nearly everything is PLAY

If we don't step in too quickly to resolve minor disagreements, we allow our children time to practise conflict resolution and negotiation skills.

Nature play
- Provides connection with the natural environment.
- Promotes observation skills and curiosity.
- Good for mental health.

Digital play
- Encourages problem-solving and critical thinking.
- Promotes creativity.
- Develops digital literacy.
- Benefits depend on the quality of the content and how it is used.

Free play
- The ultimate in play.
- Can include any type of play.
- Unlimited benefits!

Most types of play don't need expensive toys; in fact, using their imagination and 'object substitution' adds an extra benefit to many types of play.

The ability to use 'pretend' objects is an essential step in play development. Imaginative play lights up the brain!

Preferred play

Some children prefer solitary play, while others prefer to be more social. Some love active play and never stop – and others prefer quiet activities. And this is all okay! At different ages and stages, children will engage in each type of play in different ways. Not only will their stage of development influence this, but so will their preferences, their need to process events in their life and the influence of their playmates. Whatever their preference, play is essential for their development. Concerns about a child's development may arise if they enjoy a very limited range of play and their play is repetitive. If you observe this, it is advisable to seek professional advice.

The answer to nearly everything is PLAY

Providing play opportunities

Unleash the contents of your linen cupboard to become a secret cave, a magical kingdom or the mechanic's workshop.

Some parents may think they cannot afford the toys needed for 'educational play'. However, please be assured that imagination and creativity, rather than money, make for great play. Kitchen cupboards and drawers provide musical instruments such as saucepans and spoons. They also offer resources for scientific experiments, including containers, funnels, cups, straws – and food colouring if you are adventurous. Linen cupboards restrain sheets that are just itching to be great cubbies, forts or castles when they are combined with unsuspecting chairs or tables. Play with water and sand, or even dirt, provides valuable sensory experiences. Visiting the park offers opportunities for social, physical and adventurous play or even a nature scavenger hunt. Going bush has many benefits for children and adults alike! So many free options!

Busy work and home lives can make it challenging for parents to find time to play with their children. When parents are stressed, burnt out or time-poor, they often resort to technology to occupy their children so they can complete chores and claim some time for themselves. Unfortunately, this means they miss the joys of connecting with their child through shared fun. It also means the children learn to opt for easy entertainment rather than engaging in other play activities themselves or with their siblings.

On the other hand, in an effort to provide their young children with a head start, some parents devote a lot of time to educational games and programs at the expense of free play. While these children may show development in the target areas – such as cognitive and language development – they may miss out on the types of play that aid the development of social and physical skills and emotional regulation.

A balanced approach is needed, where children get enough connection with their caregivers, enough freedom to use their imagination and direct their own play, and enough opportunities to engage in various play types.

Seeking help for parenting or mental health concerns is essential, so you can be the parent you want to be for your children.

Chores

This is a little sidetrack at the end of this chapter to give a few words on chores and how meaningful participation in them is beneficial to children's wellbeing and development. While the focus of this book is play, a sense of belonging to the family is essential – and a part of this is participation in family life. Through helping with household chores and activities such as gardening and baking, children experience Adler's Crucial Cs (Bettner & Lew, 1989). They **connect** and feel they belong by doing a task either with you or for you. Their self-esteem grows, and they feel confident and **capable**. Participation in household chores makes them feel that they **count** and that their contribution to the family is valuable. Doing chores stretches their view of what they can do – and this then builds their **courage** to do new things. Doing chores together can be fun and playful; they teach children to be helpful, and they aid development!

It may seem easier to do chores by yourself, but there is a real benefit in children participating in this part of family life.

Adler's Crucial Cs:
- To connect
- To feel capable
- To know they count
- To have courage.

Bettner & Lew, 1989.

References

Bettner, B. L., & Lew, A. (1989). *Raising kids who can.* Connexions Press.

Howard, J., Jenvey, V., & Hill, C. (2006). Children's categorisation of play and learning based on social context. *Early Child Development and Care, 176*(3-4), 379–393. https://doi.org/10.1080/03004430500063804

CHAPTER 2

Pregnant and playful

As we get older, we often stop playing – which is unfortunate, as play and its close cousin, playfulness, continue to benefit us throughout life. While this book focuses on play for children to aid their healthy development, we all know that their development begins long before birth and science tells us it is influenced even before conception. So, let's look at how playfulness can be beneficial in pregnancy.

There is increasing evidence showing that changes in the pregnant mum's hormonal and immune function as a result of chronic stress affect the brain and behaviours of the baby (Lautarescu et al., 2020). We cannot avoid all stress; indeed, avoiding all stressful situations would not be beneficial. Through manageable stress levels, we push ourselves to do new things and gain the resilience we need to cope with the ups and downs of life. However, toxic stress negatively affects both mum and bub.

The answer to nearly everything is PLAY

It is powerful, and sometimes overwhelming, to consider that what your baby is exposed to while still in the uterus can affect their development. This is not just from environmental pollutants or the impact of alcohol or drugs. The whole idea that we can pass trauma and/or strength and resilience on, not only through the environment we provide but also biologically, is quite mind-blowing. It reinforces that communities and health systems caring for mothers are vitally important. It also reinforces the value of self-care.

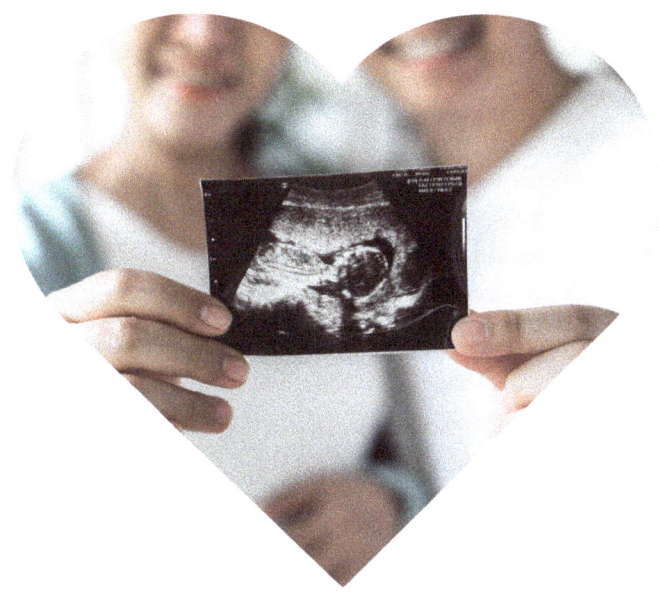

Doing the best we can

If we can give our babies the best environment for development before birth, they have a head start in life. While we have no control over many aspects of life, there are also many we do, and we can target these. I firmly believe that everyone does the best they can with their available resources. These resources may be support, knowledge, accommodation options, or good health and mental health. A lack of any of these resources can make doing the 'right' thing very hard. While circumstances will mean that not everyone can achieve these goals, here are some suggestions for a healthy pregnancy for mother and baby.

Eat a healthy diet, drink plenty of water, exercise regularly and get adequate sleep.
- Start with these basics of healthy living. These are essential for physical and mental health.

Avoid all alcohol and non-prescribed drugs.
- These can harm the developing baby in many ways. Foetal Alcohol Spectrum Disorder (FASD) is very real and impacts many families. Dad and family members can help Mum by showing their support in a practical way and also avoiding alcohol and drugs.
- There is evidence that chronic alcohol use can damage the DNA integrity of the sperm (Amor et al., 2022). So, Dad avoiding alcohol before the couple try for a pregnancy is also important, especially if he has been part of the widespread drinking culture that exists in Australia and elsewhere.
- If alcohol use is an issue, seek help. It can be challenging to give it up if this is something you have used as a coping strategy – but there is help. Stopping at any stage may decrease the risk or lessen the extent of the impact on your baby's development.

FASD is a lifelong disability

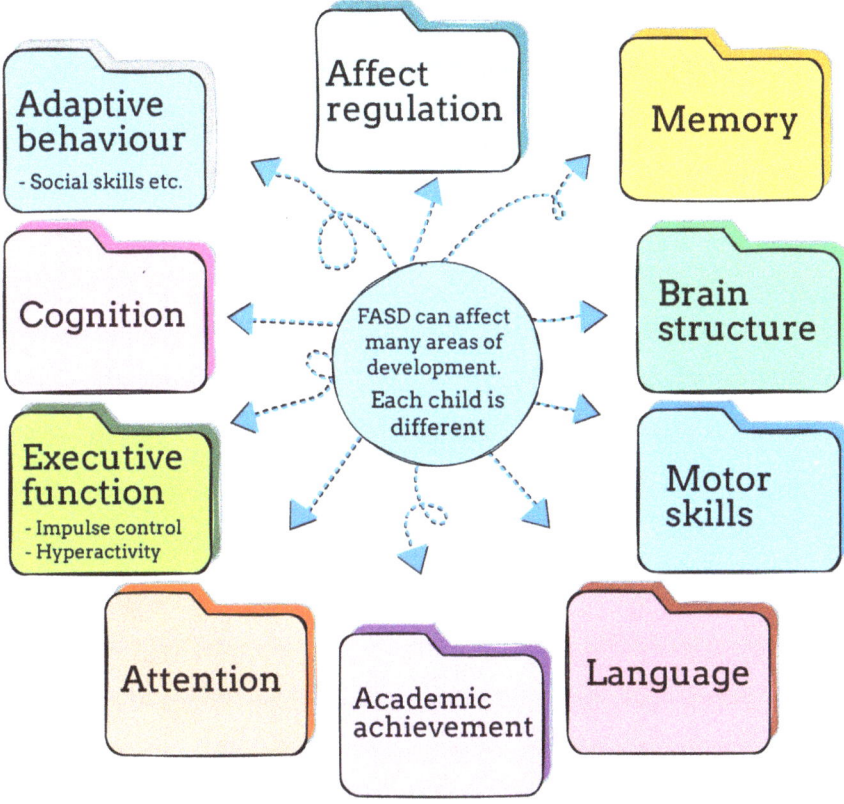

Not drinking alcohol during pregnancy is the safest option for your baby. If you were unaware you were pregnant, stopping once you know reduces the risk. If it is hard to stop drinking, support is available.

Talk to your healthcare providers if you are concerned.

Avoid cigarette smoking or smoke-filled environments.
- Smoking impacts your baby's development. The earlier you can stop smoking, the better, but giving up at any stage of your pregnancy will benefit your baby. Again, seek help. You do not have to do it on your own. These are coping mechanisms and giving them up is hard.

Seek help for any mental health conditions or unresolved trauma.
- If a parent has poor mental health, it affects their ability to parent in the way they would like to. Unresolved trauma can be inadvertently passed to your child. Your struggles can be transmitted biologically and through the environment and mood within your household.
- Addressing any historical or existing concerns while you are pregnant can give you and your growing family a great start. This applies to both Mum and Dad.
- Did you know that dads can suffer from postnatal depression, too? Keep this in mind after the birth of your child.
- Your GP is a great place to start seeking help, as they can refer you to an appropriate service.

Pregnant and playful

You don't have to do this alone.

In a crisis, call 000.
It is a crisis if you do not think you can keep yourself safe.

Otherwise, you can seek help or a referral through your GP.

There are also phone and online chat services such as:

Pregnancy Help: Ph 1300 139 313
Beyond Blue: Ph 1300 22 4636
and
Lifeline: Ph 13 11 14

Have regular antenatal checkups.
- At your antenatal check-up, be honest about how you are feeling. While these people are professionals and can often read body language, if you insist you are okay, they cannot do much to support you in a meaningful way. Let them in and let them help.

Leave domestic violence situations.
- Pregnancy can be an especially risky time. I know leaving is much easier said than done; sometimes, it can be as unsafe as staying. However, as well as the physical and mental risk to you, the constant flow of stress hormones through your body also flows to your baby and may alter their development.
- A baby exposed to domestic violence will experience trauma. The old thinking that they are too young to remember has been proved wrong. They will feel unsafe

> at a time when safety and connection are essential for their healthy development.
> - Help is available through DV Connect, 1800 RESPECT, your local GP, midwife, social worker, mental health professionals, the local hospital and the police.

Practise mindfulness.
> - Mindfulness can help you through tough days, but it needs to be a regular practice if you want to call on it when stressed. Adding it to your life while pregnant will benefit you and your baby.

Most importantly ... have fun and enjoy life!

Do not feel shame or embarrassment about seeking help before or after your child's birth. Seeking help takes strength and courage. If changes are needed, it is never too late in your pregnancy to make them; these changes will make a difference for your baby. Even if your baby has some struggles, early identification of issues will ensure the best outcomes for the child.

While playfulness, and indeed self-care, will not be a magic answer to all your problems, and 'toxic positivity' can be almost as overwhelming as toxic stress, they can help you cope with the everyday stress of life. For the bigger stuff – seek help. The good news is that even if this sounds like woo-woo, you don't have to be a believer for it to work. Just try it! Did you know that a playful approach to life can change how you perceive the inevitable difficulties encountered and your ability to cope with them – and that playfulness can be learned at any age (Clifford et al., 2024)?

Pregnant and playful

With this in mind, here are 40 activities that can aid your move towards playfulness – one for each week of your pregnancy. Some will not connect with you, but they may get your creative juices flowing, and you can make your own list.

Forty weeks – forty playful activities!

If appropriate to your situation, do activities that you and your partner can enjoy together. If not, do your own thing and love it. Many of these activities are free – or you can adapt them to be free or low-cost. Always consult your doctor before starting a new exercise program, and prioritise safety, comfort and fun!

1. Go for a scenic hike. Check out waterfalls or your favourite hiking track. Breathe in all nature has to offer.
2. Visit an art gallery or museum. You will soon be collecting the work of your aspiring artist, so now is a good time to increase your critiquing skills!
3. Go to a comedy show (or watch one on TV at home) and enjoy a good belly laugh. Laughter is a great stress reliever.
4. Enjoy an art class with a friend or be artistic (or messy) by yourself.

A playful approach helps you cope with the stresses in life!

The answer to nearly everything is PLAY

5. Have fun and relaxed date nights.
6. Play board games or video games together. Clarifying the family rules for UNO can be helpful in years to come!
7. Take a cooking class with your partner or try new recipes at home. Find delicious and nutritious recipes that you enjoy. Quick and easy recipes will also be helpful shortly. Experiment!
8. Have a movie marathon at home – or aim for a half marathon if this is more realistic!
9. Keep a diary of your pregnancy. This can just be writing three words that capture your day. Reflecting on the ups and downs in future years can be interesting. As wonderous as it is, being pregnant is not all a barrel of laughs – and that is okay!
10. Enjoy a long, bubbly bath with candles and music.
11. Write a letter to your unborn baby expressing your love and excitement as you wait to meet them.

12. Play your favourite music and dance! Notice how your unborn baby responds to the different sounds and rhythms.

13. Take a baby or phone photography class so you are an expert on baby photos when your little one arrives. There are often cheap introductory classes online. You don't need to get sucked into the next offer if you do not want to.
14. Start a baby book that includes pregnancy scans and photos.
15. Prenatal yoga or exercise classes are a good way to exercise and connect with other mums-to-be.
16. Decorate the nursery. You could make something for your baby's room, such as a mobile or a rug. Remember how quickly babies grow before you spend too much on furnishings for little ones. Also, remember how much time they will spend in *your* room. Second-hand items, so long as they are safe, are a great option.

17. Create playlists of relaxing music yourself or with your partner. This could be useful during labour – or after a hard day. Trying to find the right music when stressed can add to the overwhelm. Have go-to playlists.
18. When you wake up, enjoy your garden or yard. Go for a walk outside and survey any changes. Enjoy it at this peaceful time of day. For extra daring, go out in your PJs and enjoy your tea or coffee there. There is something wonderful in challenging conventions, even in little ways!
19. Have a pre-baby getaway.
20. Go for an evening walk with a friend (or by yourself) and enjoy the 'golden hour'.

21. Plant some flowers.
22. Learn a lullaby from another culture so you can share it with your baby.
23. See pictures in the clouds with your partner, friend or family member, assuming your part of the country is not in

drought. In this case, looking for clouds would be downright depressing! Skip this one!
24. Stargazing. This can be a mindfulness activity or a new interest. Apps can introduce you to a whole new world!
25. Go camping – commune with nature.
26. Have cereal for dinner. Who says you have to follow the rules all the time? Be a rebel!
27. Have a campfire. Stare into the fire and see what images you can see.
28. Cook marshmallows or chocolate bananas on the fire. You need to practise these skills!
29. Have a baby shower and play silly games.
30. Smell the roses and dance in the rain – literally!
31. Check out an abstract art class online. There are often free introductory ones.
32. Play with a pet.
33. Start a vegetable garden. Pumpkins and tomatoes are pretty easy!
34. Dance while sweeping, mopping or raking. This may make some people wonder about you, but your baby will appreciate you practising! They will love you dancing with them.
35. Have a mocktail evening. There are some great recipes for these, and remember, Ms Google is your friend when you don't know something. Just don't believe what they say about the important stuff.
36. Read a funny or light-hearted book.
37. Ring a friend who makes you laugh. Keep your connections. Be aware that a partner limiting your connections is a red flag for domestic violence.

The answer to nearly everything is PLAY

Maintaining your connections is essential for your wellbeing. A partner limiting your connections is a **red flag** for domestic violence.

38. You could clean the kitchen cupboards while listening to your favourite music. Alternatively, skip the cleaning and listen to the music! You do you!
39. Increase your doodling skills. Check out neurographic art. Yes, it is a real thing! Again, Google is your friend.
40. Finally – and maybe this should have been the first one. Start a gratitude practice for your family. This type of practice can change our lives by altering our perspective. See the fun, see the good. This does not mean you are oblivious to the hard stuff or that it is any less – but you know that the 'good' exists alongside it. 'This is sad' and 'I am grateful for you being here'. What a great gift for your child as they start their journey in life.

Preparing to play with your baby

Play and playfulness during pregnancy are important for another reason. For various reasons, some parents struggle to play with their children. It may be because they were not played with when they were young, they may have experienced trauma or had life experiences that shortened their childhood, or it may just be something they did not enjoy. Play, however, is a crucial way to connect with your child and is necessary for their development. So, increasing your comfort with playing and being playful will help you as you enter the exciting world of being a parent.

Support

13YARN: 139 276 is an Aboriginal and Torres Strait Islander crisis support line. It is available 24 hours a day, seven days a week.

1800RESPECT: 1800 737 732 is the national online and telephone counselling and support service for people who have experienced or are at risk of experiencing sexual assault and/or domestic and family violence. It is available 24 hours a day, seven days a week in Australia.

Beyond Blue: 1300 22 4636

Lifeline: 13 11 14

Perinatal Anxiety and Depression Australia (PANDA) Helpline: 1300 726 306

Pregnancy, Birth & Baby: Phone 1800 882 436 to speak with a midwife or maternal child health nurse from 7 am to midnight (AET), seven days a week.

Pregnancy Help: 1300 139 313

References

Amor, H., Hammadeh, M. E., Mohd, I., & Jankowski, P. M. (2022). Impact of heavy alcohol consumption and cigarette smoking on sperm DNA integrity. *Andrologia, 54*(7), e14434. https://doi.org/10.1111/and.14434

Clifford, C., Paulk, E., Lin, Q. et al. (2024). Relationships among adult playfulness, stress, and coping during the COVID-19 pandemic. *Current Psychology. 43*, 8403–8412. https://doi.org/10.1007/s12144-022-02870-0

Lautarescu, A., Craig, M., & Glover, V. (2020). Prenatal stress: Effects on fetal and child brain development. In A. Clow & N. Smyth (Eds). *International Review of Neurobiology*. (Vol. 150, pp. 17-40). Academic Press. https://doi.org/10.1016/bs.irn.2019.11.002

CHAPTER 3

Connect the dots

Brain development

Oh, my goodness! Your child is born! The world has changed and will never be the same again! Your baby will rock your world in many ways and for many years to come! So, let us start at the beginning and look at what is needed for the best possible development of this tiny person you have brought into the universe.

Your baby's brain starts to develop in the first couple of weeks after conception. By the time they are born, they have about 100 billion neurons, and their brain is about a quarter the size of an adult's. Your baby's brain will grow at an extraordinary rate. By the time they turn one, it will have doubled in size and by the time they are three, it will be about 80% of its adult volume (Zero to Three, 2022). As well as growing in size, it rapidly creates connections, or synapses, between these neurons.

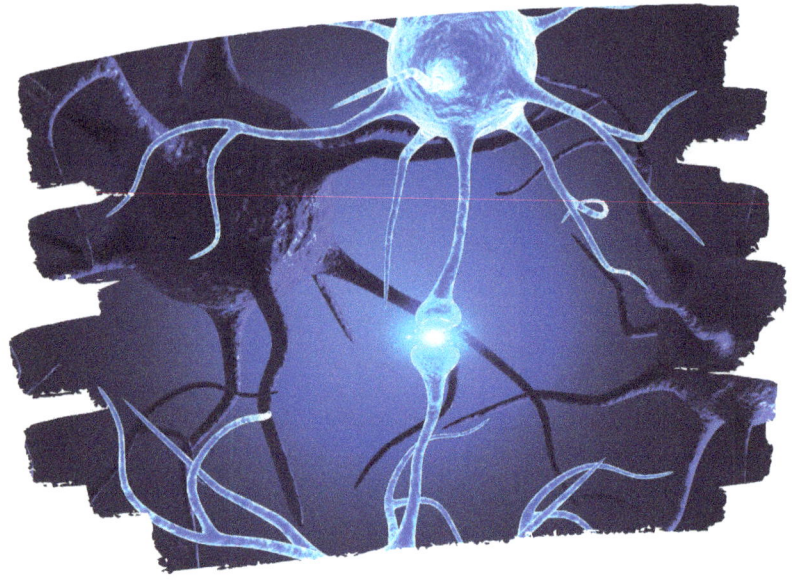

While genetics provide the basic wiring diagram, the baby's environment and experiences are heavily involved in constructing the vast network of neurons and synapses that will make up your baby's brain. How this network is wired will influence how the brain processes the information it receives. Our babies are totally dependent on us, and what we provide emotionally, physically, socially, culturally, spiritually, etc., will influence how they connect the dots. Let's make it the best dot-to-dot it can be!

The brain stem

The brain develops from the bottom up, so the first part of the brain we will look at is the brain stem. The way we divide the functions and the timing of the development of the different parts of the brain is somewhat artificial. Brain functions require an infinitely complex network of components, and development happens

Connect the dots

before and after the given timeframes. However, the bottom-up model provides a way to understand the brain-building process and what we can do as apprentice electrical engineers in this project. Apprentices, as we are all learners here! Each child, each brain and each parent is different. No one person has all the answers. Don't get sucked into the idea that there is one parenting guru. From each person offering advice, you need to consider the information and determine what may work for you and your family.

The brain stem forms about six or seven weeks after conception and then continues to develop and mature before and after birth (Prayer et al., 2006). How awe-inspiring is that? A couple of specialised cells meet somewhere warm and cosy – and BAM! A pregnancy! When many first become aware they are pregnant, a little brain is already starting on its developmental journey.

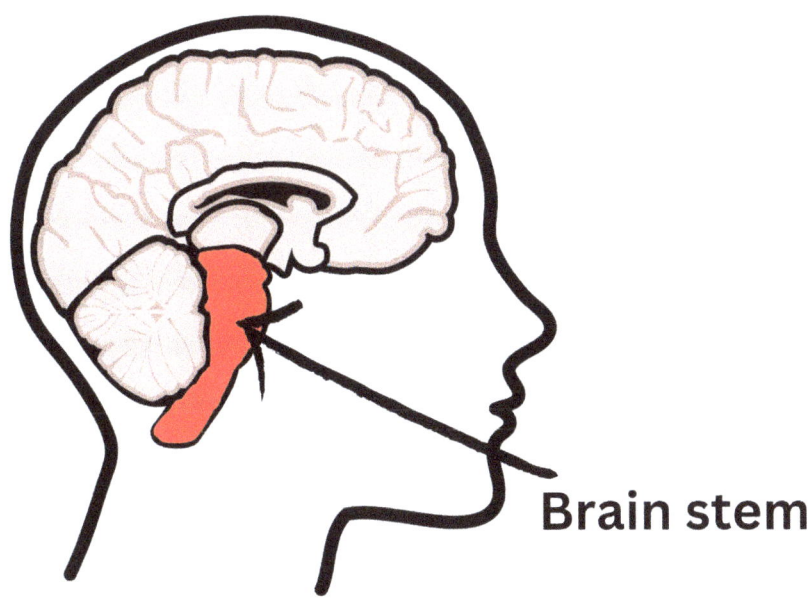

Brain stem

The brain stem is located at the base of the brain, and it connects the spinal cord to it. While significant development starts during pregnancy, after birth, the most active growth occurs between zero and nine months (Perry, 2006). The brain stem controls all our vital functions: breathing, heart rate, swallowing and body temperature (Perry, 2006). It also plays an essential role in our level of arousal and consciousness. Arousal refers to how energised we feel. Lower arousal levels reflect tiredness, boredom or sadness; higher levels indicate excitement, aggression or anxiety. In addition to these vital functions, the brain stem is like the highway at rush hour, carrying motor and sensory information back and forth. If this is not enough to convince you of the importance of the brain stem, it is also associated with our survival modes: fight, flight, freeze or collapse.

Meeting the baby's physical and safety needs and providing connected and attentive care are essential to healthy brain stem development (Perry, 2006). While it is not impossible to change and redirect the wiring later – it is much more complicated when all those other components are connected. All future development is linked to this early wiring.

Initially, your baby is utterly dependent on you and is adapting to life outside the womb just as much as you are adjusting to having a newborn. The environment and experiences you provide will shape the foundations of their world.

Connect the dots

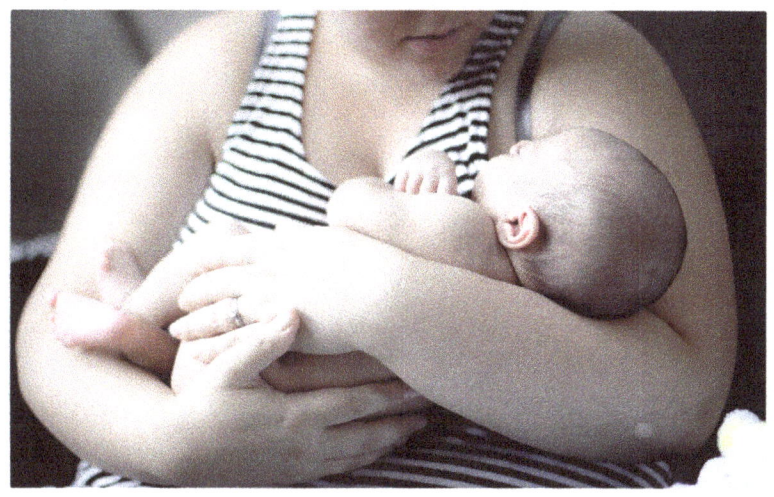

You are my world!

Survival tactics

Babies are infinitely clever and quickly learn a survival tactic or two. By six to eight weeks, they will learn to use strategies to engage a caregiver. They will coo and smile and generally be cute. Looking at this quite cynically, these actions are designed to train the carer – to ensure that they will meet their needs and protect them. When we respond to the baby's cries and do our best to figure out what they want, the baby learns that the world is a safe place with people who will love and protect them and respond to their physical, emotional, social and growth needs. This provides them with life-long benefits.

Some days, parenting will feel like the most fantastic experience on earth – while on other days, it will just be overwhelming. This is normal. Remember, your baby needs a good enough parent — not a perfect one. However, if you are struggling, make sure you seek assistance. No-one is judging, and other mums and those who work in this area know that seeking help is the most courageous act.

- You could phone your partner, your Mum or a friend.
- You could phone your midwife, child health nurse or GP.
- Or phone Pregnancy, Birth & Baby 1800 882 436.

Recognising postnatal depression and anxiety and seeking help early provides the best outcome for Mum, the baby and your relationships. It is also important to recognise the impact of a new baby on dads — remember, they can suffer from postnatal depression, too.

If a baby's physical or emotional needs are repeatedly unmet, they may experience toxic stress. Some babies may persist in crying to get a caregiver to meet their needs; others may initially cry but eventually give up and become quiet and withdrawn as they learn the crying strategy does not work. These are adaptations that they learn to aid their survival. These strategies may replay as they get older, even though they may no longer be necessary or appropriate.

Calm down!

You will remember from earlier in this chapter that the brain stem is associated with levels of arousal. This knowledge is helpful as it means we can purposefully up-regulate or down-regulate our children and our households, i.e. either calm them down or energise them using developmentally appropriate activities from this list or elsewhere.

This knowledge is also valuable for understanding that when we are upset (i.e. aroused in technical talk), we operate in the lower brain regions, restricting our access to problem-solving thinking. Stress hormones such as cortisol and adrenaline are released when we are distressed, and our bodies and brains need time and space to recover from this influx of chemicals. Our kids are no different, and their brains are still developing. They too need time and space to recover from emotions such as anger, frustration, disappointment and sadness.

Have you heard the saying, 'Never in the history of calming down has anyone calmed down by telling them to calm down'? But we all do it! Repeatedly!

The answer to nearly everything is PLAY

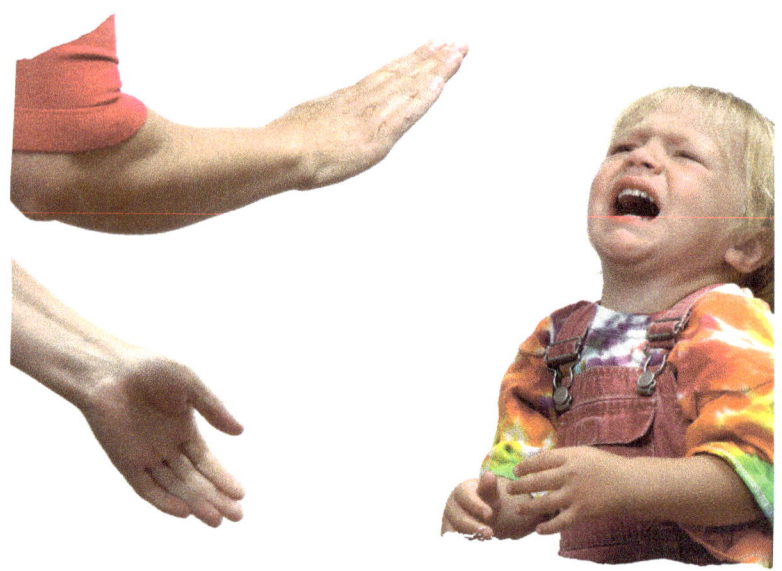

Bruce Perry gives us the 3 Rs (Regulate, Relationship, Reason) as a three-step way to manage emotions. First, we need to regulate ourselves and then our child, then repair the relationship, and finally, we can reason with them. We often intervene when we are dysregulated and demand calm, or we force our calm and try to reason. We know neither works, so it is worth giving this approach a try. It takes practice, but it is definitely worth the effort.

The first step in regulating is acknowledging the feeling. You would be surprised how effective it is to say, 'You are really upset because you have to pack up your game now. I know it can be hard when you are having so much fun. Would you like a hug, or shall we sit here a while?' Often, the child does not think you 'get' how they are feeling and will keep ramping up the behaviour until you do. By acknowledging the feeling, you are letting them know you understand. You are helping them to regulate – and repair the relationship.

Young children, and some adults, do not have the words or skills to express their feelings, especially when upset. This does not remove rules or boundaries – it just means that you talk about it when their brains can take that information on.

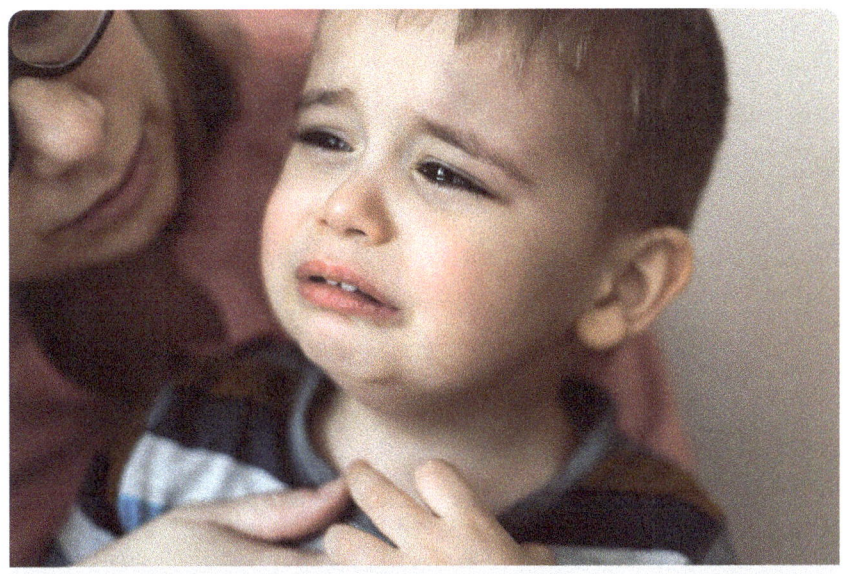

REGULATE - RELATIONSHIP - REASON
(Perry, 2024)

Bruce Perry, in Brainstem Soothers (2024, p.2), tells us that brain stem regulating activities need to be:

- *Relational (i.e. offered in a safe relationship)*
- *Relevant (i.e. matched to the child's development rather than their age)*
- *Repetitive and predictable*
- *Rewarding, fun and pleasurable*
- *Rhythmic and resonant with neural patterns*
- *Respectful of the child, family, culture, etc.*

The list below provides ideas for activities that regulate and support the development of the brain stem. As you can see, many are everyday activities and things that many people do naturally with their babies and children. As mentioned earlier, when choosing activities, it is essential to remember the stage of development rather than age. As skills develop on the foundation of earlier skills, it is important that learning is taken one step at a time. And remember to keep it fun and playful!

Activities to support bonding, early development and brain stem soothing

Many of these activities support multiple areas of brain development so will feature again in later chapters.

1. Rocking is calming for both Mum and baby. It is interesting to note that the speed of rocking often matches Mum's heartbeat. If Mum is stressed, this may be too fast to settle the baby. If you can purposefully slow the rocking, that will help, or if you slow your breathing, you will calm, and your heart rate will slow. If possible, give your baby to someone else to rock for a while and have a break. You are already Super Mum! You do not need to take on everything.
2. Cuddling is essential for connecting and bonding. This close physical contact promotes a sense of comfort and trust, and future relationships are built on the foundation of this initial bonding.
3. Patterned massage with a soft and gentle touch is magic. It is calming, sensory and connecting.

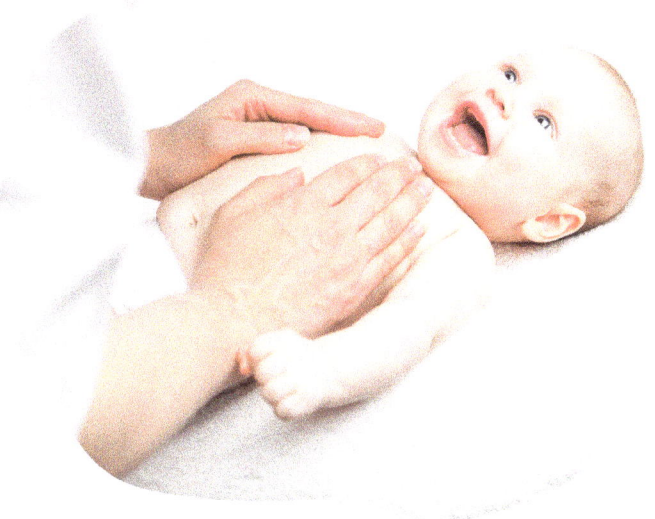

4. Wrapping your new baby snuggly but not too tightly can help them feel secure. It mimics the confined environment of the womb and reduces the startle reflex that can wake them. If the weather is hot, use very light material.
5. Bathtime can be lots of fun. It provides sensory input while providing a sense of safety and connection.
6. Singing or talking softly is soothing and reassuring for your baby. Your voice has been a constant since before they were born.
7. Face-to-face interaction is essential for bonding and a sense of security. Maintain eye contact, smile and talk to them. Spend time mirroring your baby's expressions and gestures. This back-and-forth interaction is called 'serve and return' and is essential to brain development and bonding.
8. Position your baby so they can see mobiles. Bright colours or black and white work best for younger babies. This provides visual stimulation.

9. Tummy time gives your baby different sensory stimulation and helps motor and muscle development.
10. Play games like 'this little piggy', where you gently squeeze each toe in turn. This increases body awareness and connection.
11. Offer soft, textured toys and toys that make sounds. This expands your baby's sensory horizons.
12. Read aloud to your baby. This is beneficial even before they understand stories. A bonus benefit is that reading aloud requires controlled breathing which can be calming for the reader – and your state of calm is catching!
13. Play 'pat-a-cake'. The repetitive hand movements and the rhythm of the song help improve coordination and strengthen the bond between you and your baby or toddler. You can play 'pat-a-cake' in the sand as well as it being a clapping game.

Pat-a-cake, pat-a-cake, baker's man,
Bake me a cake as fast as you can.
Pat it and prick it and mark it with a 'B',
And put it in the oven for baby and me!

The first record of this rhyme is in 1698!

14. Making sandcastles is a great sensory experience!
15. Movement songs like 'Row, Row Your Boat' and 'When All the Cows Were Sleeping' provide rhythm and movement.
16. Water play or playing in the mud can be both calming and exciting!
17. Shaving cream art is messy, sensory fun!
18. Bubble wrap stomp is repurposing at its best!
19. Copying rhythms using fingers, spoons or sticks is easy and fun and creates a feeling of being 'as one'. You can also do 'call-and-response' activities using claps, stomps and finger snaps.
20. Tapping (EFT) is a fantastic regulating strategy for children (and adults).
21. Cover a balloon or bowl with paper mâché and decorate. It is sensory, messy and creative!
22. Work together in the garden. Shovelling and raking provide 'heavy work' and rhythm.
23. Baking provides sensory input (touch and smell) and builds a connection to the person doing it with them.
24. Skipping has a great rhythm, and children often do it in connection with others.
25. The rhythmic motion of swinging can be calming and help regulate emotions. It can also be fun and connecting.
26. Modelling with playdough or clay is sensory and calming.
27. Swimming has excellent benefits with its controlled breathing and rhythmic movement.
28. Walking and running both have their rhythms – and multiple benefits for physical and mental health.

The answer to nearly everything is PLAY

29. Create sensory trays with your choice of materials: rice, goop or different fabrics. Rice with lavender oil or colours can stimulate additional senses.
30. Play with Kinetic Sand. Children enjoy exploring the different properties of this type of sand.
31. Hand clapping games, such as 'Miss Mary Mac', etc., involve rhythm and connection.
32. Message massage: Draw a letter or shape on their back and ask them to guess what it is. As they get better at it, try a word.
33. Jumping on a trampoline, with age-appropriate safety measures, is fun and rhythmic and expends excess energy. Many children find this a calming activity.
34. Do kid's yoga poses together. A yoga dice can make this extra fun!
35. Drumming is a great rhythmic activity that can be used to express emotions.

36. Do a 'magic' body scan. Start at the head and slowly scan the body for hot areas, cold areas, sad areas, jiggly areas, etc. Pretend it is an alien scanning your body to see what is happening!
37. Blowing bubbles requires breathing to be regulated, and thereby regulates the nervous system.
38. Singing, humming and reading all need breath control. Our breathing becomes fast and shallow when we are stressed or anxious. All of these activities can help slow and deepen the child's breathing without giving direct instructions. Put on some music and sing!
39. Music and dance are fantastic. They can increase energy or calm the body and brain. If trying to change a child's 'state', the trick is to meet them where they are with energy levels, then gradually slow or quicken the beat.
40. Riding a bike. The constant circular motion of the feet can be very calming for the brain.

References

Perry, B. (2006). The neurosequential model of therapeutics: Applying principles of neuroscience to clinical work with traumatised and maltreated children. In N.B. Webb (ed), *Working with Traumatized Children in Child Welfare,* (pp 27-52). Guilford Press.

Perry, B. (2024). *Brainstem soothers: Helping a child's brain and body learn they are safe.* Beacon House Therapeutic Services and Trauma Team. https://beaconhouse.org.uk/resources/

Prayer, D., Kasprian, G., Krampl, E., Ulm, B., Witzani, L., Prayer, L., & Brugger, P. (2006). MRI of normal fetal brain development. *European Journal of Radiology,* 57 (2). 99-216 https://doi.org/10.1016/j.ejrad.2005.11.020.

Zero to Three. (2022, May 18). *22 Statistics you need to know about brain development.* Zero to Three. https://www.zerotothree.org/resource/distillation/22-statistics-you-need-to-know-about-childhood-brain-development/

CHAPTER 4

The cerebellum and diencephalon

These vital brain parts have really weird names, and you might be tempted to skip this section because it sounds too technical, but they are just names, right? We could rename them Sara and Di, perhaps?

The first of these two, the cerebellum (Sara), is located just above the brain stem (let's call him Barry) and toward the back of the brain. Our friend Sara is responsible for balance and coordination. Her functions also include voluntary motor movement, muscle tone and equilibrium. However, she shares this responsibility with other parts of the brain.

The second, the diencephalon (Di), is located between the brain stem (Barry) and the cortex. These relationships are starting to sound dodgy! The diencephalon is vital in relaying and processing sensory and motor information. It is also involved in managing emotions.

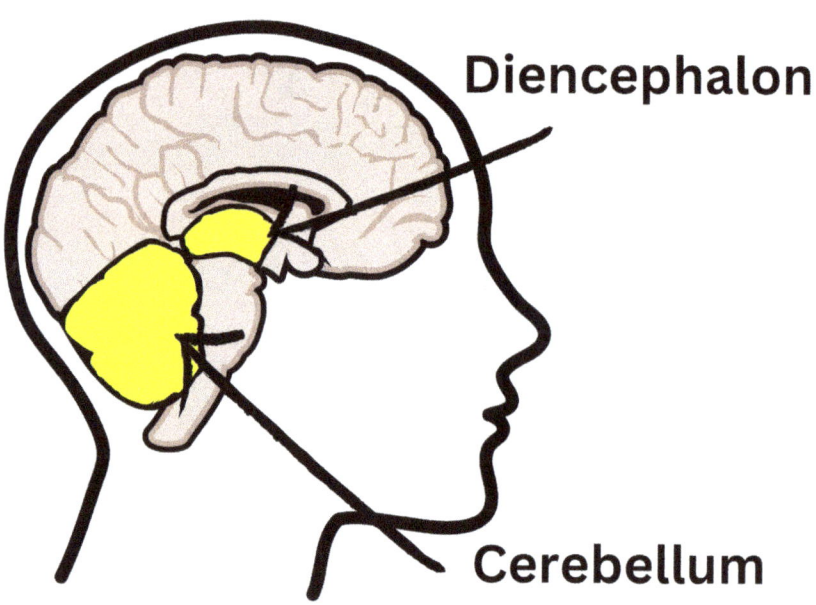

The most active growth period for the diencephalon and the cerebellum is from six months to two years (Perry, 2006). At this stage of brain development, promoting a feeling of safety and connection and providing a range of experiences that use all the senses is crucial (Perry, 2006). Physical activity is also essential for developing this part of the brain (Perry, 2006).

Physical development

You will notice that this stage of development (six months to two years) corresponds to your baby starting to crawl — and then progressing to walking, running and climbing. They are developing all the skills they need to move faster than *Flash* and escape as efficiently as Houdini! Keeping up with them can be hard work; however, if a child is left in its cot for too long, they have little stimulation, which may affect the development of this part of the brain. Of course, there will be times when you need a bit of a break, and their cot may be the safest spot for them for a short time. If the cot or a playpen is placed in the area where the family is, it can allow your baby to interact, use their muscles and see the household's activities. It can let you get things done, keep your baby safe, and still provide stimulation. It is also important that a baby does not spend too much time restrained in a walker, jumper, etc., as full movement is essential for muscle growth, balance and brain development.

Active play's role in physical development

Running, jumping and climbing benefit your child's physical and mental health. Below are some of the areas of physical development that active play benefits.

Gross motor skills
- Play activities like running, jumping, climbing and swimming help build muscle strength and endurance.
- Coordination and balance are improved through throwing, catching, kicking and balancing activities.
- Play requires all sorts of weird and wonderful movements that improve agility and flexibility.

Fine motor skills
- Activities like building with blocks, doing puzzles and playing with small toys improve hand-eye coordination.
- Manipulating objects during play develops fine motor skills and dexterity.

Bone and muscle development
- Physical activity helps build stronger bones.
- Engaging in active play promotes muscle growth and development.

Sensory development

During this same period (six months to two years), the senses also go through a rapid stage of development. Our senses are much more than the five we generally consider: hearing, sight, smell, touch and taste. Some other senses are proprioception, interoception and the vestibular system.

Proprioception allows us to know where we are in space. A child with trouble processing proprioceptive stimuli may have poor body awareness and motor planning, poor postural control, and sensory-seeking behaviours. Some examples of this may include pressing so hard on their pencil that the lead breaks, having difficulties walking up and down stairs, slumping and often moving in their chair, difficulty balancing on one foot and chewing their clothes or other non-food items.

Interoception is the sense that lets you feel and understand what is going on inside your body, such as whether you are hungry, your heart is beating fast or your muscles are tense. This sense is involved in self-regulation. Often, people with anger management issues who report going from '0 to 100' without noticing have trouble feeling what is happening in their bodies.

The answer to nearly everything is **PLAY**

The *vestibular system* allows us to coordinate balance and movement. Children with processing challenges related to the vestibular system may be sensitive to, seek out, or be slower to respond to vestibular input. Those sensitive to vestibular input may avoid using swings and climbing on playground equipment; those seeking vestibular input may be unable to sit still or persist in rocking their chair, a common issue in classrooms. A child with difficulty processing vestibular input may quickly lose balance and appear clumsy.

If a child has problems processing their senses, an occupational therapist is the best person to assist. If you are worried about your child's development, you should always seek professional help.

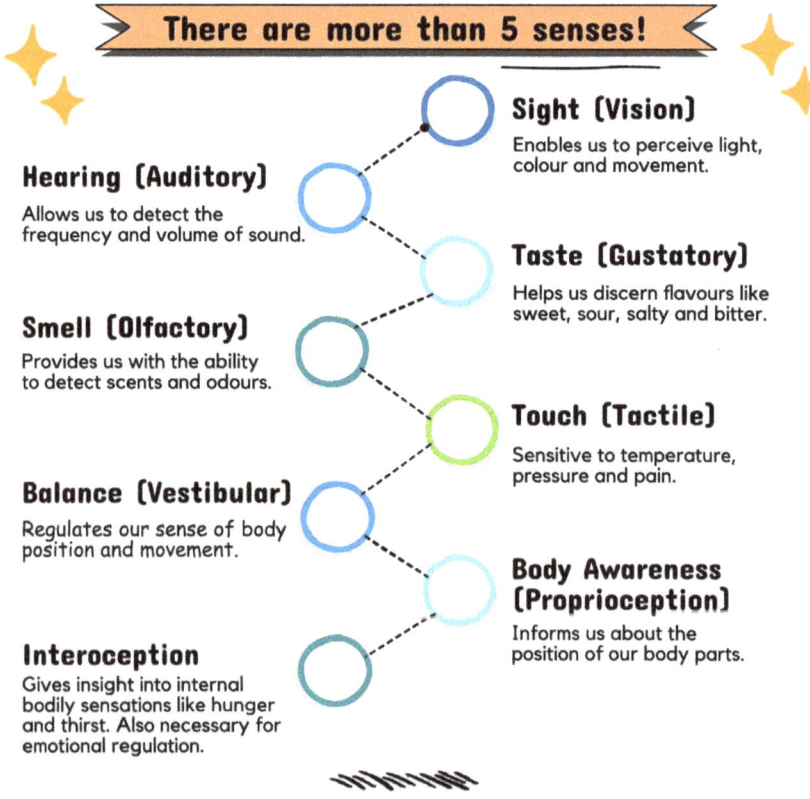

There are more than 5 senses!

Sight (Vision)
Enables us to perceive light, colour and movement.

Hearing (Auditory)
Allows us to detect the frequency and volume of sound.

Taste (Gustatory)
Helps us discern flavours like sweet, sour, salty and bitter.

Smell (Olfactory)
Provides us with the ability to detect scents and odours.

Touch (Tactile)
Sensitive to temperature, pressure and pain.

Balance (Vestibular)
Regulates our sense of body position and movement.

Body Awareness (Proprioception)
Informs us about the position of our body parts.

Interoception
Gives insight into internal bodily sensations like hunger and thirst. Also necessary for emotional regulation.

Babies need opportunities to experience their world through all their senses.

Play's role in sensory development

So many of a child's needs for healthy development are met through their everyday activities and play. It is fascinating, however, to know how and why these simple things benefit our children. This knowledge helps us know we are doing the 'right' thing and giving our children the best opportunities – especially if they struggle with developmental issues.

Some of the ways that play supports sensory development include:

Sensory stimulation
- Children's play often involves multiple senses, such as sight, sound, touch, taste and smell. This stimulates numerous areas of the brain and helps build neural connections.
- Children learn to tell the difference between different sensory inputs, such as noticing the differences in textures, sounds or smells.
- Play helps children process and combine information from the different senses. This is called sensory integration.

Sensory processing
- For children with sensory processing differences, play can allow them to seek the sensory input they need. This might include swinging, spinning, enjoying the sensation of rubbing a particular texture of material between their fingers or playing with water.
- On the other hand, play can also help children gradually tolerate sensory stimuli they may find overwhelming. Some children may find loud noises, bright lights, movement, touch or food textures overwhelming.

The challenge is working out what makes each child tick, what makes them shine and what overwhelms them.

Adapting play for children with sensory processing difficulties

There is no instruction manual accompanying any child's arrival, but when a child has sensory processing difficulties, even play can present a range of challenges that can leave you wondering what to do.

When reading these suggestions, remember that every child is different. Also, each child may respond differently on different days, depending on how tired they are or how close they are to sensory overload. Nonetheless, here are a few ideas for adapting play activities to suit children with sensory processing difficulties.

Firstly, we must understand the child's needs. Observe them and pay attention to their reactions to different stimuli. What bothers them? What do they enjoy? An occupational therapist can help you create your child's sensory profile, which can help guide what you can try.

Some of the ways activities can be adapted include:

Control sensory input
- Auditory: If noise is a problem, try providing noise-cancelling headphones, earplugs or a quiet space.
- Visual: Reduce visual clutter, use dim lighting, and reduce time spent with a visual focus.
- Tactile: Offer alternatives like gloves, tools or different textures.
- Vestibular: Start with gentle movements and increase.
- Oral: Offer different food textures and avoid overstimulating flavours.

- Olfactory: Keep them away from or avoid strong scents that they find overwhelming. This may include perfumes or cooking aromas.

If a child has sensory challenges, occupational therapists can recommend the appropriate sensory supports.
Sensory supports could include:
- Noise-cancelling headphones
- Visuals
- Fidgets
- Weighted toys/blankets
- Wobble cushions
- Pressure-vests
- Calm spaces
- Regular timed breaks
- Chews/chewing gum
- Theraputty
- Alternative seating
- 'Heavy work'
- Movement breaks.

Provide choices
- Allow them to choose the activities, toys or materials they prefer. This fits with the principles and benefits of free play.

Create a calming environment
- Use soft lighting, calming colours and gentle music.
- Calm adults and calm voices also help.

Offer sensory breaks
- Encourage the child to take short breaks from overwhelming stimuli. Sensory overwhelm accumulates, so allowing space to lower these levels regularly can prevent a meltdown. Meltdowns are distressing for the child as well as the carers.

- You empower the child to care for their own needs by encouraging self-initiated breaks.

Incorporate sensory activities
- Provide opportunities for sensory input that the child enjoys. This may be water play, jumping on the trampoline, hanging upside down on the climbing frame or squishing play dough.

Examples of adapted play

- A child may want to use gloves to play with play dough, finger paint or to play in the sand. A simple adaptation like this can make an activity they did not want to do enjoyable and accessible.
- When playing outdoors, sunglasses and a hat can reduce bright light. Playing outside in the evening is another option.

- If going on family adventures, start with short times and give the child all the details well beforehand so they know the duration and location. This reduces anxiety about it being more than they can handle.
- A child might enjoy swinging and climbing but struggles when there are a lot of children and noise. Taking them to the park in quieter times will be much more enjoyable.

You know your child best, and with some imagination and professional advice, you can find a range of ways to work with your child's strengths. Even though you may want to fill developmental gaps, it is really important to keep in mind your child's strengths and preferences while you do this. Forcing a child to engage in play that overwhelms their senses will not end well and can cause harm. Play must always remain fun!

Activities to support physical and sensory development

Again, many of the activities listed are things that we would typically do with children of this age, and many overlap with those from the brain stem chapter. In the brain stem chapter, the focus was on their value in bonding, rhythm and regulation – and now we see they also benefit balance and coordination. Feelings of safety and connection continue to be crucial throughout life. The brain stem, cerebellum and diencephalon all form part of the sensory highway, so overlapping activities aid their development.

Catch me if you can!

1. Tummy time helps build muscles and allows the baby to experience the world differently. Reaching for favourite toys encourages further muscle development.
2. Rattles, drums and bells allow babies to explore different sounds.
3. Soft toys with different textures stimulate the sense of touch.
4. Rolling a ball or a car back and forth requires many motor and planning skills, and they need to trust that you will return the object.
5. Having the space and freedom to learn to crawl, sit up, stand up and then walk are essential activities for healthy muscle, bone and brain development.
6. Waterplay soothes the body and brain and engages the senses. If you and your baby are having a difficult day, adding water may be the solution; whether it is a bath, the hose or a toddler's pool, it can really improve everyone's mood!

7. Action songs continue to be important for many reasons, including muscle development, coordination, connection and language development.
8. Shape puzzles strengthen visual discrimination and spatial reasoning and help develop fine motor and problem-solving skills.
9. Playdough or clay provides great sensory play while also developing muscles and fine motor skills.
10. The 'freeze' dance game improves coordination and impulse control. In this game everyone dances until the music stops and then freezes.
11. Playing tag is an excellent way for children to exercise, improve coordination and learn social skills like taking turns, following rules and accepting being out.
12. Play 'keep it up' with a balloon. It's fun and is exercise for developing bodies. It supports muscle and bone development and increases balance and coordination.
13. Free play outdoors is essential for children's development in all areas, especially their physical development.
14. Hide-and-seek is a great active game that encourages problem-solving and helps develop spatial awareness. 'Can I fit in there? Will they see me?'

Catch me if you can!

15. Hand-clapping games have multiple benefits, from improving coordination to increasing connection. They are also fun and regulating.
16. A 'follow the string' maze will challenge balance, coordination and problem-solving skills. It could be over the lounge, under the table, around the chair, etc. It could end with a snack together out under a tree.
17. Arts and crafts activities such as painting, drawing and making things develop fine motor skills while allowing creative expression. Using plastic tweezers to pick up beads or art supplies is a great activity for fine motor skills.
18. 'Walk like this' or 'animal walks' use different muscles and require coordination. A bonus is that if you tell a reluctant toddler, 'Let's walk to the car like an elephant' or 'Let's jump like frogs to the bath' you will get less pushback. If you engage their sense of fun, life is much easier for everyone.

19. Breaking bubbles is an awesome activity. It can spark lots of physical action even before your child can blow them themselves.
20. Climbing, balancing and swinging help with the development of balance and coordination.
21. Twister is great for kids – and for your flexibility!
22. Jumping on a trampoline helps develop muscles, balance and coordination.
23. 'Simon says' helps with coordination and following directions. It also helps create the space between thinking and doing, allowing us to plan our actions rather than react, i.e. practise impulse control.
24. Juggling requires good hand-eye coordination, focus and quick reflexes. Start with one ball, then two (Ms Google can give you instructions if this is not in your skill set!). Some kids find this too frustrating, but some who struggle with other things find their strength in circus skill activities. This is great for their self-esteem and often gains them respect from their peers.
25. Have a dance party you design or use Just Dance or similar. Dancing is a fun way to improve coordination and fitness and is also great for connection.

26. Hopscotch improves coordination and balance. Drawing with chalk on the cement adds to the fun – and the benefits.
27. Throwing and catching a ball improves hand-eye coordination and timing.
28. Skipping is a fun way to improve coordination, balance and cardiovascular health. You will notice skipping also popped up in brain stem activities. It is one of the all-round good guys!
29. When old enough, skateboarding or rollerblading extends balance, coordination and motor skills.
30. Bike riding is great exercise and requires balance and coordination.
31. Tai chi is a mind-body exercise that improves flexibility, balance and coordination.
32. Yoga can help children improve their body awareness, coordination and focus. While there are special kids' yoga groups, there are also many free offerings on YouTube.

33. Duplo, Lego or other building blocks encourage spatial reasoning and help develop fine motor skills. They also promote creativity and problem-solving.
34. As children get older, engagement in sporting activities has many physical and wellbeing benefits.
35. Playing a musical instrument requires coordination, fine motor skills and auditory processing.
36. Walks in nature use all the senses and encourage exploration.
37. Obstacle courses challenge a child's balance, coordination and motor planning. These can be inside or outside. Inside, you could create an obstacle course using chairs, cushions, boxes, blankets, etc.
38. 'I spy with my little eye ...'. For younger children, this can be something blue or something round rather than a letter. It can help improve visual processing, focus and memory. Bonus info: Simple actions like looking for five things that are blue and four things that are square are good 'grounding' activities if a child is anxious.
39. Matching games help with visual discrimination, problem-solving skills, memory and concentration. Who would have thought a simple game of snap or a game of memory could do so much? And then there is the benefit of having an adult give them their undivided attention while they do it (if possible). This is so valuable!
40. Swimming is an excellent exercise for strong muscles and good coordination. Another all-round good guy.

References

Perry, B. (2006). The neurosequential model of therapeutics: Applying principles of neuroscience to clinical work with traumatised and maltreated children. In N.B. Webb (ed), *Working with Traumatized Children in Child Welfare* (pp27-52). Guilford Press.

CHAPTER 5

Giggles and goosebumps

The limbic system

Deep in the brain, just above the brain stem and below the cerebral cortex, is a group of structures called the limbic system. This sounds like the instructions to find the hidden block of chocolate you have kept in the freezer for emergencies! At times, that block of chocolate may be needed! This chapter can be a bit heavy and emotional as we may recognise our own traumas and triggers, but understanding our reactions and what we can do about them is so important. On the other hand, we may be pleasantly surprised by glimmers from our past. So, keep that chocolate handy in case – and I promise we will get to the fun and games part.

The limbic system is associated with our behavioural and emotional responses. It includes some more weirdly named components: the hippocampus, the amygdala, the thalamus and the hypothalamus.

Together with other parts of the brain, the limbic system is also involved in processing memories and providing motivation.

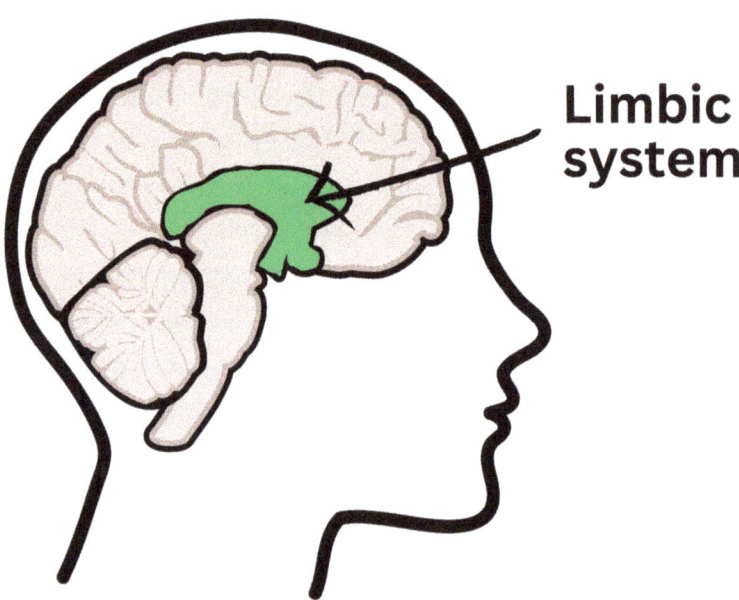

So, what do these bits do?

The *hippocampus* is integral to learning and remembering new information. It is the part of the brain that helps us form new memories and recall old ones, especially those related to our personal experiences and emotions. The hippocampus also links sensations (such as smells or sounds) to our memories, which is why a scent or a song may trigger a memory or an emotion.

Head trauma, age, stress and disease can damage the function of the hippocampus. Exercise, managing stress levels (for ourselves and our kids), and treating mental health issues can help keep the hippocampus functioning well. It is also important to wear seatbelts and helmets to protect the brain from injury. The hippocampus is especially vulnerable.

The *amygdala* is the part of the brain that regulates our emotional responses, such as fear, anger and happiness. It also attaches emotional meaning to our memories and is involved in our social interpretations. It is probably the most well-known component of the limbic system, as it is involved in our fight-or-flight response and is essential to keeping us safe. It constantly watches for things that may be a threat to us and prepares our body to respond.

However, in adults and children who have been impacted by trauma, their amygdala may become overactive, and they may feel the need to fight or get out of the situation – even though they are safe. This response may be an adaptation that has kept them safe in the past but is not helpful now. It can be stressful and exhausting when you see the world as a dangerous place. When a child is hyper-alert or easily dysregulated, we must be curious why. They do not choose to be this way. If we are similarly affected, seeking mental health support is really important.

Violence in the home makes children feel unsafe. Their lives are scary and unpredictable.

This affects how their brains develop and can have lifelong consequences as their brains prioritise survival over normal development.

Children exposed to violence will often have social, emotional and behavioural problems.

A safe environment is essential for healthy brain development.

The answer to nearly everything is PLAY

When the amygdala has been triggered in response to a perceived threat, it activates the body's response through the autonomic nervous system. In preparation for fight or flight, hormones are released into the bloodstream, increasing alertness, heartbeat and blood pressure. Breathing becomes more rapid and shallow. Blood is pumped to the muscles. This is all to prepare you for action that will keep you safe. Unfortunately, our body interprets the 'threat' of a traffic jam and being late to work the same way as if you saw a woolly mammoth charging toward you. If someone has been exposed to trauma, it may only take a smell or a sound to trigger that response – leaving all those around wondering what happened.

In today's hectic lifestyles, it is not uncommon for our nervous systems to perceive constant threat, and a small incident can escalate very quickly.

When we are fully in fight or flight mode, our logical, problem-solving part of the brain becomes disengaged, and we react to the threat rather than thinking our actions through. For real threats, this is awesome – for others, it can be problematic.

The good news is that, although it may be a difficult and painful process, healing from trauma is possible. We can learn ways to 'calm our amygdala' and put space between an event and our (re)action. Many of the activities in this section aim to do this.

The *hypothalamus* controls many vital functions, such as body temperature, hunger, thirst, sleep and hormone production. It is also involved in regulating our mood and sexual arousal. No wonder these are closely linked!

The *thalamus* processes sensory information such as hearing, taste, sight and touch. It is also involved in emotions, memory and planning.

Most active growth 1 – 4 years

The limbic system's most active growth occurs between one and four years (Perry, 2006). As it is responsible for our emotional responses, behavioural regulation and connection to others, its healthy development determines how we interact with the world and others. Attachment, social language development, empathy, tolerance and interpretation of nonverbal language are also associated with the limbic system. Positive, safe experiences during this time of rapid development provide a foundation for future relationships (Perry, 2006; Hong & Mason, 2016). While each area of the brain has some involvement with emotional regulation, the limbic system is particularly important.

Developmental trauma

Developmental trauma is when the developing brain has been overwhelmed by neglect, abuse, separation or exposure to violence in the home. It can significantly affect the limbic system, resulting in a range of difficulties. Babies and young children are particularly vulnerable to trauma that is repeated and inflicted by people they trust.

Impaired wiring
- Research shows that children and adults who have experienced trauma often have impaired wiring in the brain's limbic system. This can lead to issues such as anxiety, depression and difficulties with self-regulation (Evergreen Psychotherapy Center, 2023).

Stress hormones
- Trauma alters stress hormone levels, which impacts the developing brain and body.

Emotion regulation
- The prefrontal cortex helps us control our feelings. However, exposure to adverse experiences when we are young can interfere with the function of this part of the brain (D'Orazio, 2016).

Where the healthy development of the limbic system has been disrupted by trauma, it is essential to create safe environments, build positive relationships and address cognitive difficulties to help these children achieve their potential.

'Relationships heal relationship trauma.'

Dr Karen Triesman

The activities in this section have been divided into two parts: activities that support developing emotional regulation skills and activities that support social skill development. However, again, there are many overlaps.

One of the most important things to remember is that we are constantly modelling emotional regulation to our children by how we respond to other people. This also applies to how we treat our children. They learn from what we do.

How play supports emotional development

Play is a powerful tool in supporting emotional development.

- It provides a safe space for children to express feelings, whether they are negative or positive.
- Through imaginative play, children learn to understand and share the feelings of others, which is crucial for developing empathy.
- Play helps children develop the language to describe their emotions.

- Play allows children to practise coping with frustration, disappointment and other difficult emotions.
- Overcoming challenges in play helps children develop resilience and problem-solving skills.
- Success in play contributes to a positive self-image and improves confidence.

Children learn problem-solving skills through play if we don't rush to help too early. Give your child time and space to work it out for themselves. If they can't manage, provide strategies for problem-solving rather than doing it for them.

How play supports social development

Social play is essential for developing skills to help children get on in the world. Through social play, children learn about:

- Teamwork, cooperation and compromise
- Sharing toys, ideas and experiences
- Empathy
- Taking turns, having patience and playing fairly

- Listening to others and having respect for their ideas
- Interpreting non-verbal language
- Self-regulation and conflict-resolution.

They also extend their vocabulary and often learn skills from other children. With their peers, they will usually be braver when trying new experiences than they would be with you standing close by. They feel your anxiety, and this can limit their courage.

Wow! With all that learning happening through play, they should be doing it every day! Social play is often 'free play', so it has all those bonus benefits as well.

You will notice the overlap between activities that support the limbic system and those from the lower regions of the brain, especially the earlier ones. The development of all regions of the brain connects, but there are especially close links between the brain stem and the limbic system in our acute stress response. Healthy social and emotional development occurs in the context of safety and connection, so these elements remain very important and are included again briefly.

Activities that support emotional development

1. Responsive caregiving is again a priority for development. Responding promptly to your baby's cries, providing comfort and meeting their needs helps build a sense of security and trust, which is essential for emotional wellbeing throughout life.
2. Gentle touch and cuddling reappear on this list for good reason. Physical contact, such as gentle touch, cuddling

and holding, helps create a sense of security for the baby. Feeling safe is essential to healthy emotional development.
3. Play soft sounds or soothing music in the background while you are doing your usual daily activities or when your baby is resting. Calming sounds can have a positive impact on everyone.
4. Sing lullabies or simple songs. Your voice is calming and reassuring to your baby. Revisit the one you learnt from another culture while you were pregnant.
5. The value of face-to-face interactions cannot be overstated. Make eye contact, smile and talk to your baby. These interactions contribute to the development of social and emotional communication and connection.

Safe
♡
Secure
♡
Connected

6. While reading books is also a cognitive activity, a person reading to them using facial expressions and an expressive tone is a way children are introduced to a range of emotions. This broadens their exposure to emotional experiences.
7. Combine music and movement. Play music and dance with your baby. Calming music and gentle movements can help soothe and relax your child, while faster music can excite them.

8. Play mirroring games. Copying your baby's sounds and facial expressions helps them start to understand emotions.
9. Games of peek-a-boo help your baby to begin to understand what is called 'object permanence'. This means understanding that objects or people are still there, even if they can't see them. This is important for developing a secure attachment. Secure attachment can help prevent separation anxiety.
10. Puppet play, in which puppets can be anything from a popsicle stick to a really fancy one, allows children to act out stories and explore emotions.

Peek-a-boo! I love you!

The answer to nearly everything is PLAY

11. Emotion charades can be fun. Players use facial expressions and actions to portray different emotions for others to guess. Having a list of emotions can help them broaden their emotional vocabulary. Adults run out of options quite quickly, too! Many of us have quite a limited range of words for emotions. You would be surprised how many there actually are. There are about 3000 in English. This is good info for your next trivia night!
12. Play win-lose board games like Snakes and Ladders and Candy Land. This allows children to experience what it feels like to win and lose while being supported in managing feelings of disappointment or elation in socially acceptable ways.
13. Games like Jenga involve anticipation (and fear) of the tower falling. Experiencing this feeling can allow kids to use some strategies for managing anxiety (e.g. stopping, taking a breath, thinking about the worst thing that could

happen – and how they could manage that. They can also practise positive self-talk like, 'I can do this').
14. Practise relaxation techniques through fun activities like blowing bubbles or pretending to be a calm ocean.
15. Do yoga poses together.
16. Pretend play and role play allow children to experience different perspectives and the emotions that another person may feel.
17. Hide-and-seek helps develop emotional regulation and social skills. First, players need to manage their excitement when trying to remain hidden. Then, they need to manage their disappointment if they are found quickly.
18. 'Simon says' is an excellent game for kids to learn to put a gap between sensory input (what they hear) and their actions (act rather than react).
19. Completing puzzles can help build frustration tolerance.
20. Art in any form is a great way to express emotions. Examples include painting, drawing, expressive dance, drama and photography.

Activities that support social development

All the early development activities listed in the other chapters are essential for social development. These include gentle touch and cuddling, singing to your child, peek-a-boo and mirroring. Tummy time has extra social benefits if you or others are on the floor with the child.

The answer to nearly everything is PLAY

Attending playgroup has lots of benefits for both Mum and Bub.

21. Visit a friend or attend a mother's group or playgroup so your little one can socialise with other babies.
22. Group singing and movement activities help children learn to interact with others. Songs with actions or dances provide opportunities for children to follow instructions, take turns and engage in synchronised activities, promoting social bonds. These activities may be offered through libraries, play groups or community centres.
23. Blowing and chasing bubbles is lots of fun. Laughter and joint attention help with bonding. Young children may not be able to blow bubbles, but they will love chasing them! This simple and inexpensive activity aids development across all domains and is fun for parents and carers, too.
24. Outings to the park provide many benefits to adults and children. Not only is there the benefit of the great outdoors, but it also allows children to connect with other children in a neutral space. They start to learn to negotiate the use of shared equipment and learn skills by copying other children.

25. As they get older, building blocks or other construction toys provide opportunities for children to work together to build structures or create imaginary worlds. Construction play with their peers or siblings promotes teamwork, problem-solving and fine motor skills. Remember, however, that working cooperatively is still a developing skill – and that playing side-by-side on different projects and having the occasional argument about the piece they want is entirely normal.
26. Plan a group scavenger hunt where teams work together to find hidden clues and complete tasks.
27. Clapping and rhythm games, particularly when in a circle, provide a sense of belonging and group cohesion. These games have many other benefits, but socially, the sense of fun and being in sync with everyone else is very powerful.

28. Building a fort or cubby together helps develop cooperation and negotiation skills. Blankets, chairs and other materials could be used to construct the fort.
29. Plan an obstacle course where teams work together to overcome challenges and reach the finish line. If there are fewer people, it could be a team of two, e.g. Mum and one child on one team, Dad and the other child on the other.
30. Children can create puppets and perform a puppet show together. This activity requires sharing ideas and cooperation.
31. Charades or Pictionary are great social games for kids.
32. Outdoor activities such as tag, hide-and-seek or simple ball games are great for building social skills. These games provide opportunities for social interaction and help children learn about cooperation and fairness.
33. In dramatic play or role-playing activities, children can act out different social situations, which will help them understand other perspectives and gain empathy. Swapping roles in play can be helpful and insightful.
34. Memory match games and Go Fish provide practice in remembering information. They also help develop social skills, such as the ability to win and lose and frustration tolerance.
35. UNO is always a favourite. As kids play various versions at school, agree on the rules first.
36. Reading provides exposure to different perspectives and different ways of interacting.
37. Group art projects are great for social interaction, sharing and creativity. Whether it's painting, crafting or building something together, children learn to express themselves, negotiate ideas, and appreciate the diverse perspectives of their peers.

38. Organised team sports like soccer, basketball or T-ball help children learn to work together, share responsibilities and communicate effectively with their peers. Team sports also give children a sense of belonging and teach important values like teamwork and sportsmanship.
39. Working individually on a jigsaw puzzle promotes development in various areas, such as fine motor skills, visual perception, spatial reasoning, etc. Doing a puzzle with others adds social skills to the list.
40. Dancing, music, drama or other special interest groups have many social benefits.

References

D'Orazio, S. J. (2016). Assessing the impact of adverse childhood experiences on brain development. *Social Sciences, Arts & Humanities, 8*(7). http://www.inquiriesjournal.com/articles/1429/assessing-the-impact-of-adverse-childhood-experiences-on-brain-development

Evergreen Psychotherapy Center. (2023). *Attachment, trauma and the developing brain.* https://evergreenpsychotherapycenter.com/attachment-trauma-developing-brain/

Hong, R. & Mason, C.M. (2016). Becoming a neurobiologically-informed play therapist. *International Journal of Play Therapy, 25*(1),35-44. https://doi.org/10.1037/pla0000020

Perry, B. (2006). The neurosequential model of therapeutics: Applying principles of neuroscience to clinical work with traumatised and maltreated children. In N.B. Webb (ed), *Working with Traumatized Children in Child Welfare* (pp27-52). Guilford Press.

CHAPTER 6

Fact and fiction

We've reached the top part of the brain, the cortex. It is the brain's outer layer and has a wide range of responsibilities. No wonder it flips out at times! The cortex is responsible for our thinking, reasoning and creativity. It is also responsible for essential skills such as paying attention, making decisions and planning. And then there's more! The cortex is also where we process social and emotional information. So, whether it is a fantasy tale (fiction) or studying astronomy (fact), the cortex is there!

The answer to nearly everything is PLAY

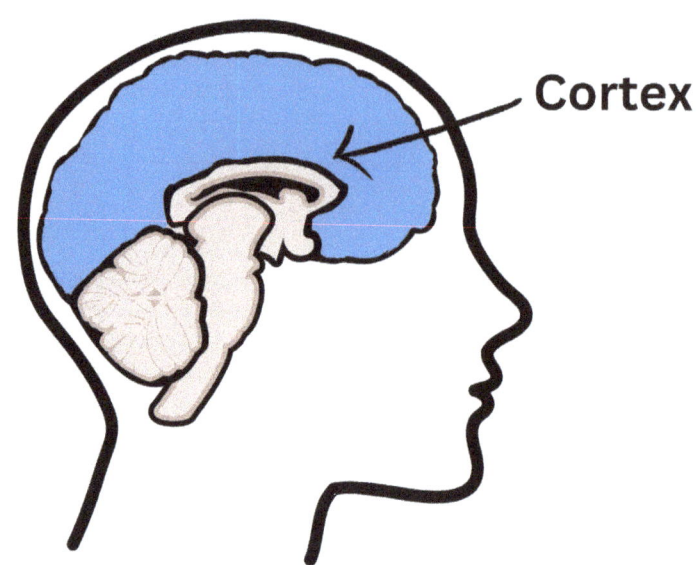

The cortex's most active growth period is between three and six years; however, it continues to develop into the mid-20s. The cortex remains able to grow and change throughout life, enabling us to learn new skills and ways of thinking. Healthy development of the cortex depends on the earlier needs being met and continuing to be met. The most important of these needs, apart from those for survival, are a felt sense of safety and connection.

While still within the range of typical development, many children in their early years of schooling will struggle with what we expect from them – just because their brains are not yet sufficiently developed. Executive function skills are necessary for success at school, and these are at the very early stage of development. You may need to get your chocolate out again! This is an area I am passionate about!

So, what are these mysterious executive functioning skills that people talk about? Are you ready for the list? Executive functioning skills include:

- Planning
- Time management
- Task initiation
- Organisation
- Problem-solving
- Flexibility
- Working memory
- Emotional control
- Impulse control
- Attentional control
- Self-monitoring.

It is quite a list! While all this development is taking place in the early years of schooling, it is in no way complete.

Impulse control is needed to sit still or stay in a line; attentional control is required to copy something down from the whiteboard; and emotional control is necessary to handle not getting your own way. As you can see, these are important for learning and complying with expected classroom behaviours.

For some children, not complying may mean that their brain development is just not there yet. Formal preschool often expects more than normal development allows, and then people wonder why the child is 'difficult'. It is our system that is difficult for the child. I love the idea that the school should be ready for the child rather than the child being ready for school.

For other children, developmental delays, trauma, cognitive impairments and/or neurodiversity can further compromise their ability to conform and learn. These issues are often not diagnosed

The answer to nearly everything is PLAY

early, and vulnerable children frequently end up having (or being labelled with) behavioural and emotional problems.

Providing access to play is the most significant thing we can do to aid brain development for children. As mentioned earlier in this book, it is through play with their peers that they learn social skills, problem-solving, conflict resolution and emotional regulation. Through play, they can also process their emotions and the events in their life. This may be the death of a pet, the birth of a new baby or going to school. I have noticed in my work that when children start wanting me to be a student, and they be the teacher, their learning really goes ahead. They are ready to learn. Often, before they reach this stage, they struggle.

The benefits of play are innumerable. Children enter a world of imagination where they learn to make up a story and figure out how to communicate that to another. This will translate into being able to narrate and write a story. They learn how far they can push one another and also practise nurturing and protective roles.

Fact and fiction

Play's role in cognitive growth

As you have seen in the previous chapters, play has benefits linked across all domains and areas of brain development. However, there are some particular benefits for cortical development.

Enhances cognitive functions
- Play often involves overcoming challenges, which strengthens problem-solving skills.
- Imaginative play encourages creativity and thinking outside the box.
- Remembering rules, strategies and sequences in games helps develop memory.

Helps develop executive functions
- Children often plan their actions during play, developing their ability to strategise.
- Games with rules help children learn impulse control.
- Keeping track of multiple elements in a game improves working memory.

Helps with language development
- Social play encourages the use of language.
- Creating stories and characters during pretend play expands vocabulary and communication skills.

'Nothing lights up a child's brain like play.'
Dr Stuart Brown MD

The answer to nearly everything is PLAY

Activities that support cortical development

Early in life, activities that develop the cortex will include a baby mirroring their caregivers' smiles, the sounds they make and the faces they pull. Later, they will explore their environment through touch, putting things in their mouth, watching colour and movement, and enjoying games like peek-a-boo. These simple experiences have tremendous benefits!

Building them up is fun, but so is knocking them down!

Fact and fiction

Imitating sounds and facial expressions provide connection and are the start of communication. This face-to-face interaction is so powerful - it connects brains!

1. Stacking cups or large building blocks allows your baby to explore size, order and cause-and-effect. They can stack them and then knock them down. Building and destroying can be equally fun at this stage!
2. Your baby will need no encouragement to drop articles from their highchair. While sometimes annoying, this action teaches them about gravity and object permanence as they watch the toys disappear and reappear. This is also a baby-initiated study on cause-and-effect. Albert Einstein is reported to have said, 'Play is the highest form of research' — so it comes with a high recommendation!
3. Finger painting. Use edible finger paints for a messy and fun sensory experience. It encourages exploration and introduces basic colour concepts.
4. Shape sorters. Sorting shapes into corresponding holes can enhance problem-solving skills and help develop hand-eye coordination.

5. Making music is great for the development of all areas of the brain, including the cortex. Introduce simple musical instruments like shakers or soft drums. You can also use saucepans and a wooden spoon. This is a little less loud than an ordinary one! A BBQ sauce bottle with rice inside is also a great instrument.
6. Simple wooden or plastic blocks used to build towers and walls encourage creativity, spatial reasoning (understanding how things fit together) and problem-solving skills. They start learning about balance and gravity as they construct towers and towns.
7. Sorting and matching games. Simple sorting games using objects like colourful toys, building blocks or pegs help develop pattern recognition and classification skills, which are early math concepts.
8. Reading board books together is a beautiful way to bond with your child (or grandchild) and introduce new vocabulary. Point to the pictures and ask them simple questions about the story. Encourage them to participate with sounds or simple words. You will notice their memory at work as they start to predict what will happen and look for their favourite parts.

9. Sing action songs and recite nursery rhymes with your toddler. These fun activities help them develop memory, rhythm awareness and language skills.
10. Scribbling and drawing. Provide large sheets of paper and safe crayons or markers. Let your toddler explore the joy of making marks and lines. This activity is foundational for future drawing or writing skills and allows them to express themselves creatively.
11. Introduce simple memory games like matching cards or hiding objects under cups. These games support cognitive development by improving memory and concentration skills. Rather than helping too quickly, encourage a problem-solving approach.
12. Art and craft activities. Encourage your child to participate in more complex arts and crafts projects involving cutting, pasting and assembling. These projects promote creativity, fine motor skills and spatial awareness. They also encourage problem-solving as the child plans and then carries out their artistic creations. Craft activities have much more value when they are individual creations than when everyone does them the same way.
13. Jigsaw puzzles. Start by providing simple puzzles with only about four pieces, and then, as they master them, provide puzzles with more pieces and more intricate designs.
14. Go Fish and 'concentration' feature again, as they are great memory games that are fun and accessible.
15. Encourage imaginative play with dress-up clothes, dolls or action figures. Role-playing scenarios stimulate creativity, language development and an understanding of social behaviour.

16. Magnetic chess is a cheap, simple game that requires strategy. It also provides an opportunity for experimentation with magnets, promoting curiosity and learning.
17. Start with simple board games and, as appropriate, move to more complex games with clear rules. These more complex games will require strategic thinking, planning, and an understanding of the game's dynamics. For example, start with Candy Land or Snakes and Ladders and move to Scrabble or Monopoly.
18. Chess requires a whole new level of strategy if you are up for it. Children often learn to play rather quickly and will give you a run for your money.

19. Simple science experiments that explore concepts like mixing colours, basic chemical reactions (e.g. vinegar and baking soda), or simple physics support cognitive development by encouraging curiosity, observation and critical thinking.

They also enhance language skills as children describe their observations and experiences. Science is fun!

20. Due to the level of addiction to devices, I am a bit reluctant to add this, but I am also a realist and acknowledge their value. Consider educational apps or games that align with the school curriculum and focus on math, language or science subjects. Interactive learning through technology can reinforce academic skills in an engaging way. For some children, this provides a very valuable, alternative way to learn or reinforce their learning. Remember to monitor use – both for overuse and misuse. The value of the app will depend on its content.

21. Rough-and-tumble play has significant cognitive benefits. Children must constantly assess the situation, anticipate their playmates' actions, and adjust their behaviour accordingly. They learn to continually evaluate and manage risk. They need to regulate their emotions and be aware of their body's position in relation to others. It is a complex social and cognitive exercise.

22. Learning to play a musical instrument has many cognitive benefits!

23. Learn to dance – or even just *one* dance. Memorising and mastering dance steps requires memory, concentration and focus.

24. A Rubik's Cube provides a good cognitive challenge.

25. Walks in nature prompt curiosity and promote focused attention. They can also spark imagination and increase innovative thinking. As a bonus benefit, they reduce stress and improve mood. Take the whole family!

26. Go to a play or other performance. Following the storyline, understanding the characters and interpreting their actions

requires focused attention and comprehension. If we go further and discuss the play with our child, analysing the plot, themes and character development will stimulate critical thinking.

27. Sporting activities require quick thinking and strategic decision-making. They also require players to focus on the game, remember strategies and be flexible in their responses. This is all in addition to their social and emotional benefits.
28. Crossword puzzles improve vocabulary, spelling and logical deduction.
29. Sudoku requires logical reasoning and problem-solving skills.
30. Pictionary requires quick thinking, creativity and communication skills.
31. Coding and programming require logical thinking, planning, problem-solving and creativity.
32. Making specific shapes with a tangram requires reasoning, problem-solving and frustration tolerance!
33. Write poetry. This can give the brain a real workout!
34. Building with Lego or other small construction bricks promotes problem-solving, critical thinking, creativity and persistence. Children can either follow instructions or make their own creations. Each way of playing has its own benefits.
35. Keep a journal. It could be a written journal or an art journal – or a combination of both. Journaling has mental health and cognitive benefits.
36. Playing Charades requires imaginative ways to portray words and phrases. It also requires problem-solving skills and deductive reasoning.
37. Visiting a zoo promotes curiosity and language development. Children use focused attention as they look at the animals,

Fact and fiction

and often, their observations are even more detailed than ours. They also have fun identifying animals and recalling facts and stories long after the visit.

38. Read a range of nonfiction and fiction books or articles. Find the interests of reluctant readers, and remember that comics, magazines and anime are all books. Books offer children a door to anything that interests them. They often find things on the internet that match their interests, but be sure to give them access to books, too.
39. The game of twenty questions requires you to remember the questions asked, develop an effective questioning strategy and apply deductive reasoning.
40. Visit a museum or art gallery. They are a treasure trove of knowledge and creativity for everyone, but for visual learners, they can open new worlds.

The answer to nearly everything is PLAY

All good adventures come to an end, and we have reached the end of this tale of everyday play and all its wonders. However, that does not mean the end of brain development or the need for play and playfulness. We continue to learn new things and new ways of thinking throughout life. Play and playfulness help keep our brains and bodies flexible and ready for anything. Play on!

"We don't stop playing because we grow old; we grow old because we stop playing"

– George Bernard Shaw

About the Author

Anne Maree spent her early life in Roma before moving to Redcliffe with her family when she was in Year Nine. However, Anne Maree was not a city kid, and she left school at sixteen to return to Roma as a trainee nurse.

She is proud to be one of George and Patricia Lister's six children and knows her upbringing has allowed her to achieve her dreams, including publishing this book. Her mum's sense of playfulness and love of getting down on the floor to play with and connect with her grandchildren modelled what Anne Maree later found to be what the experts theorised about.

Anne Maree has completed a Bachelor of Social Work (Hons), a Masters of Suicidology, a Graduate Diploma in Therapeutic Play and a Diploma in Creative Arts and Health and is committed to life-long learning. She is particularly interested in neurodevelopment and play and how we can use this knowledge in our everyday interactions with children to increase their sense of safety, connection to others and development.

The answer to nearly everything is PLAY

Anne Maree is passionate about preventing developmental trauma and educating about the long-term implications of adverse childhood experiences. Her dream is that one day, we will have a much greater focus on preventing and healing trauma in our communities.

She is fascinated by the wisdom evident in First Nations' cultural practices and traditions throughout the world, which match with what neuroscience is now discovering.

Anne Maree lives in Normanton and has four adult children and a much-loved grandchild. For ten years, she provided counselling to children at schools in the surrounding area, but now she is focusing on writing books for adults and children about emotional regulation and childhood development along with completing further study.

www.ingramcontent.com/pod-product-compliance
Lightning Source LLC
Chambersburg PA
CBHW041146110526
44590CB00027B/4141